A Steppenwolf Breathes The Morning Air

Poetry, Stories And Other Prose

I0633797

Nigel Pearce

chipmunkapublishing
the mental health publisher

Published by

Chipmunkapublishing

http://www.chipmunkapublishing.com

ISBN   978-1-84991-961-6

Chipmunkapublishing gratefully acknowledge the support of Arts Council England.

Author Biography

Born into a family with profound vault lines in 1959 Nigel has lived a life both blessed and damned. Blessed because of his love of books and ideas which was encouraged but which paradoxically exacerbated the fault lines at home causing him to run away to live in counter-culture at the age of 13. A potent brew of experimental art and radical ideas lead him to try and transcend the artificial boundary between everyday life and creativity. To live a life that was an antithesis of the grey banality of suburbia. He has no regrets about the decisions he made as young person then, other than they may cause truncation of his life expectancy. The damned part followed fairly quickly, but intermittently as it so often does for dreamers of absolutes: mental illness and illicit substance dependency. However he has now been 'illegal drug' free for 29 years and has been alcohol free for well over a decade and tobacco free for around ten years. Unfortunately although abstinence has enormous benefits: academic and creative achievement the mental illness persists, if not in quite such an intense form as do physical problems related to both the medicines that were prescribed and the self-medication. Nigel has gained a B.A (Hons), Dip H.E. from the Open University and a Certificate in English Studies at Warwick University. He is currently pursuing further his academic and creative goals

It is now nine years since I almost died from a medically induced toxic state related to medicines prescribed for mental health issues. I now have had three previous books published by Chipmunkapublishing and gained two new qualifications to add to my the B.A (Hons) before the toxicity, a Certificate in English Studies at Warwick University and this year have completed a Dip. H.E. gained at the Open University. The doctors at the time thought, once I had survived the toxicity, the only way ahead would be a sort of vaguely animated death in long stay psychiatric care. I have proofed them wrong which is not to say my body and mind have totally recovered, but it illustrates that adversity can be overcome. This collection of poetry, stories and explorations of the intellect are possibly more positive, some are still quite dark but that is in the nature of my experience and writing, than the other collections. When confronted with one's mortality in a quite palpable form you either sink or swim psychologically: I swam. A desire to push the boundaries of both the creative and the intellectual is pervasive in my work and life, I know of no other Path. My writing and love of ideas is my salvation, not a pastime but a vocation.

A Steppenwolf Breathes The Morning Air

"My mind hums hither and thither with its veil of words."

— Virginia Woolf, The Waves.

The steppes had been a wasteland of significance for the Steppenwolf and some wolf packs probably had revenged his mind and body when he had the misfortune to meet them: learning his nature and accepting it on the savannahs and avoiding those marauding packs had been an important step after many false ones. The other place had its own deprivations that was where they the Worldings lived with all their concerns about banalities; no the Steppenwolf preferred the meaningful desolation and had become habituated to the solitude. For didn't he have his books and writing materials.

Whether he had been born here he had wondered much, if he had be born atoll seemed debateable at times after a particularly protracted and lonely trek when a younger wolf of the steppes. They had been a male wolf, from whom he often fled. and another called his 'mother'. The mother had taught him the ways of the steppes, herself a Steppenwolf but one made captive and taken to a cave where she was taught to speak like a Worlding but could never quite manage their language of platitudes. But, being of a similar nature, if tamed and harnessed she taught him to listen to the winds which swept across the steppes and interpret its beauty, understand its music. The tamed Steppenwolf also taught him to record the Steppes and the World in his notebooks and fashion them into poetry and prose and a love of sniffing that sharp morning breeze and opening a book.

As I observe this surreal world I shall not deceive you with his dialogues, his life is an interior monologue which from time to time others are granted access, but his observations of you and yes you are penetrating; you cannot escape those drowsy amber eyes. This world is not the physical world of Central Asia, the Steppenwolf has two rather than four legs yet it is not the green and pleasant land of those cursed with the fidgeting of the sane terrain, no this land is named by some mental illness, by others who believe, although this is by no means certain, they have a privileged knowledge of the Steppenwolf: 'Paranoid Schizophrenia.' But my acquaintance with him is one of The Omniscient Eye, not divine but one of narrator of tales, the weaver of words.

Steppenwolf was 'born to be wild' and as less the fully developed wolf was hitching down the M1, destination Notting Hill Gate. Not yet the playground of the less than totally sophisticated children of the dollar it was then a British version of Height-Ashby. First 'lift' was off a lorry driver, quite a large articulated one, that is the lorry rather than the driver who was a pleasant man of late middle-age:

'Want a lift, how old are you?'

The Steppenwolf was dressed in kaftan, jeans and beads and with a tee-shirt. He did not reveal the age of his body, but rather his mind.

'Come on get in, when did you last eat.'

'Like, is that meaningful man.'

'Here take my packed-lunch.'

6

'Thank you.' the young wolf replied for the steppes he had grown-up in where suburbia.

In fact the exodus to that part of London had in the preceding years been mainly one from affluent if stifling zones. Like the people of the Book of Exodus these young people believed themselves to be both blessed and as a consequence persecuted. all believed themselves to comprise a sort of tribe of steppenwolfs, but some were Steppenwolfs amongst the tribe, indeed would wander through magic doors endlessly with and without any assistance, no would rather tumble through them, indeed for this Steppenwolf he would walk like a somnambulist through doors and entrances and fall over precipices. At first he had not realized people will push you through doors and hurl one over the cliff edge. He had thought that this behaviour was confined to the land of the Worldings. How wrong can a young wolf setting out across the steppes from a world of yelling and threats, those are merely transformed into different matter, there can seem to be only dark matter at times, but he possessed the key to shut the doors both magic and otherwise and allow the illusion of existence to be retained. The key to freedom was the written word and the word read in a relationship with the reader however anonymous that may be.

Five years later and the wolf was wandering the plateau with a haversack and the light of the moon for guidance, the pleasures of the lunar night which are enchantment and torment each in full measure, balanced precariously like a set of scales suspended from the cloud where the memory of the trail of Socrates and the his death with a dose of hemlock are pervasive. He was an outcast but did not realize it, had embraced Harry Hiller, the Steppenwolf of Hermann's novel, as a young man but of course Harry Hiller was a middle aged man when he walked through the magic door and did not have an assortment of brightly coloured phials chained around his mind, oozing into the textures of his brain. Cast out of the wolf pack for he was a little to 'wordy' for many and not willing to act out the correct role of an albino in the specimen room for eloquent steppenwolfs. The Steppenwolf did not pursue the tarnished calve of hedonism nor could he be a shepherd for lost sheep or a matador to slay the Minotaur. He slept on people's floors and in those old crumbling Trogon Horses, the lunatic asylums.

The Steppenwolf was huddled on a park bench, the Worldings eyeing weary for its was a scorching summer's day and he was ensconced in a filthy duffle coat and a very long purple and white scarf wrapped several times around his neck, almost a sort of vestment. He was elsewhere for he was the protagonist of not one but all of Camus' novels; this was a little difficult to grasp. no certainly his mother hadn't died that morning and he hadn't experienced any kind of existential self-realization, but on that bench, day past day past day but 'The Outsider' seemed to have the clarity of a million sunrises with the dew hanging on the whispering grass. Was he Meursault, he wondered: a man of around sixty always walked his Scottish terrier through the park, past the human debris which was the Steppenwolf, by this time the odour emitting from him must have been fairly potent and have looked rather unkempt?

'My name is Monsieur Meursault and am experiencing

an existential crisis, are you acquainted with this.'

'Bloody hell, he's flipped.' and the dog yapped in agreement.

The police came and the ambulance and the nurses 'specialed', not allowing even to the toilet by himself. He refused to take off the duffle coat and the other patients and then the staff called him Paddington. He had a marmalade sandwich just after medication time brought by a Spanish nursing auxiliary Francis with a mug of Horlicks. The Steppenwolf wondered whether Francis was really Italian and from Assisi. Then a young nurse who looked like Rupert Brooke told him quietly:

'If you want to leave, you must stop this high-fluting conversation,

then the doctors will think you are better. And for god's sake stop

quoting from 'Dust' by Rupert Brooke'.

'But it is more than existence, it has essence, it gives life and death.'

He opens the book and read the lines he knew by heart:

'When the white flame in us is gone,

And we that lost the world's delight

Stiffen in darkness, left alone

To crumble in our separate night;

When your swift hair is quiet in death,

And through the lips corruption thrust

Has stilled the labour of my breath --

When we are dust, when we are dust! --

Not dead, not undesirous yet,

Still sentient, still unsatisfied,

We'll ride the air, and shine, and flit,

Around the places where we died,

And dance as dust before the sun,

And light of foot, and unconfined,

Hurry from road to road, and run

About the errands of the wind.

And every mote, on earth or air,

Will speed and gleam, down later days,

And like a secret pilgrim fare

By eager and invisible ways…

'Stop that immediately or there will be a nice little jab for you.'

The 'conditioned reflex' had been taught and 'reinforced' so many time he knew what your hospital expects every patient to do, no it was going over the top in a Flanders field to the rat tat-tat of gunfire, but the sound of breaking glass, the struggle and the jab of chlorpromazine. Pre-ordained, conditioned and stamped...

It was a cloud swept rain biting day Father was buried.

It was a cloud swept rain biting day Mother was buried.

The Steppenwolf has carefully arranged his rather abundant supply of medication in colourful piles in sequence of potency in order to make sure the clock stops. But unlike one Paddington Bear, he has cast off the civilising death giving effects of that green and pleasant land or rather the supervised walks around the green and pleasant grounds of those old hospitals and returned to 'darkest Peru' or in his case the metaphorical Steppes of his mind, he is totally alone: emotionally, intellectually and creatively and with the exception of the odd visitor physically. The choice is his, he listens to the Beethoven piano concerto No.5, the one the captive steppenwolf played endlessly in her cave to him, she had tuned him into the music of the crashing spheres, taught him to interpret it and hear it in the cold winds which sweep across those steppes and given him a key to unlock Pandora's Box but to see that it contained the good, those things he must live and write about. He tidies away the medicines and begins to write. It is 5.00 a.m. on the eighth anniversary of his mother Isis' death. The Steppenwolf goes outside and breathes the morning air and it is good.   ,

A latter-day leper

A bug was bagged just for moral sanctimony in a shop of a holy
sacred music faith,

It was a case of contagion danger so he is to be pillared as he must
be on the fiddle.

No nothing to do with appearance for they know not yes they do he
has the plague.

I have the flu so have this rather large of box of tissues I bought at
Boots just now,

We do not want any of that here they say in a jerked horror which is
spattered out,

A leper is not in a colony it is clear but is from an asylum, prison or
infections unit.

They are so pleased until the parasite speaks and is sprinkling holy
water on them,

Exchange complete, money for folk, manna for Mammon, art thou
holy hypocrite,

All are children of the bourgeois so germ smiles and says good-bye
and they reply.

This poet in amber begins to weep with ink these words for people
cut like knifes.

Nigel Pearce

Random haiku.

Dazzling ray of light

Shines, the corn bends but breaks and

A lunar sea flows.

The stars set our course

Black raven, but wild winter

Winds blow us apart.

The harvest is sown

And grows, the crop has ripened

Too soon and fruit rots.

Two Traditional Haiku[1] for 2012.

01

Sun is the fragrance

Of love breathe that sweet scent choke

And live in moonlight.

02

Cherry blossom burns

Bright for those it praises weep

We sleep in the frost.

---

[1] The essence of haiku is "cutting" (kiru). This is often represented by the juxtaposition of two images or ideas and a kireji ("cutting word") between them, a kind of verbal punctuation mark which signals the moment of separation and colours the manner in which the juxtaposed elements are related.

Traditional haiku consist of 17 morae in three phrases of 5, 7 and 5 respectively. Any one of the three phrases may end with the kireji. Haiku can therefore be said to have 17 syllables.

It should also have a kigo (seasonal reference/ literally a season verse picture e.g. cherry blossom = Spring and lunar = autumn). The majority of kigo are drawn from the natural world.

The Transformation.

That saint of sanity is trapped in a glass menagerie of sanctimonious deceit,

Until a flea has penetrated the dome and flies around in search of dog dung,

The master of platitudes swipes the irritant into apparent oblivion with a fist,

A metamorphosis takes places and the black dot mutates into a fluttering bat,

Hideous beauty is born it crawls leaving a trail of crimson slime on the floor.

Being blessed with a sound mind the saint books a check-up with Doctor Sane,

The shrink with a grin and a wink says you have found your vocation Narcissus,

To be generous I will diagnose you with schizophrenia so you better play a role,

Go and roll into the foetal position because it is medication time says that nurse,

Insanity's martyr lives in an asylum but it is dwarfed by the shrine of Absurdity.

On Ethics.

This fly was caught in webs of wonder and woe long ago a gossamer that never breaks,

The problem is the maggots are eating the fly they hungrily gorge upon a fidgeting body,

Just bloated and blue with ink of a fountain pen which was ingested and always leaked,

The pen will be forged to a scythe of Nemesis implacable avenger of Demeter's harvest,

Go to grey granite forum to discuss ethics so that Categorical Imperative is considered,

Those who dine on the fly know no duty and oblivious to any utterance of Utilitarianism,

They are neither bound by one or the other moral philosophy for have a fox conscience,

Perhaps beyond constraints of good and evil for God is Dead, too complex in this case,

The one who stole from me and that casket of family is merely a creature of Hedonism.

Buzzing blue bottle must prepare, vampire slayer's stake and hammer are now needed

It is the time to expose to light that black heart; this should have been done long before

As much too free it from that source of death-in-life and its blood sucking feed of blame.

I write in golden script the writ to summon to courts of thundering law a demon of deceit.

Nemesis': a female angel of Divine retribution. **'Demeter'**: the mother goddess associated with the harvest. **'Categorical Imperative'**: in Kantian ethics this is the absolute duty. **'Utilitarianism'**: '*The greatest happiness of the greatest number is the foundation of morals and legislation.*' (Bentham).These ethics are associated with moral results. **'God is Dead'**: '*God is dead. God remains dead. And we have killed him. How shall we comfort ourselves, the murderers of all murderers?* (thus) *'Morality...is herd-animal morality.*' (Nietzsche). '**Hedonism'**: a school of thought that argues that pleasure is the only intrinsic good.

A Steppenwolf Breathes The Morning Air

Poem of a redeemed suicide.

An angel had fallen into Grace,

      this is the damnation at the antechamber of despair,

Now beyond tepid temptations

      he stumbles through the scrub of tangled blind stares

Of willful unseeing eyes no blind stares and jealous glares of those who claim to spare,

This baptism is of sand, a font

      of dust just like those who are sieves, nothing there but Barbed wire and head holes,

      the fruitless bites of those rotten apples makes me puke

Into an abyss which is home

      I know it well, here the lotus flower blossoms at 5.00 a.m.

A poet was persecuted by the magicians of modernity the priest purveyors of psychiatry,

His persuasions are portrayed in patterns of ink which we call words, not smeared turds.

Their wands are broken on the philosopher's stone which is where the poets learn craft.

Nigel Pearce

Lines on Ovid: 'Metamorphosis: Bk VIII: 183-235.'

Those words which we had so carelessly caressed the night until night was all,

They have haunted us, exorcized, now the claw scratching burden of freedom,

Phrases so tangled up in our torments there were admissions to those asylums,

She a frost-rigid Aphrodite huddled in the corner an enigma with amphetamine,

Icarus' madness was that of a youth fleeing a flame from drunk with fire father,

Burn and get burnt, you do when you fly high and then touch the Sun to plunge,

Those potions of ascent and descent were worms in graves of a fathomless sea,

> *'Let* me warn you, Icarus, to take the middle way, in case the
>
> moisture weighs down your wings, if you fly too low, or if you go
>
> too high, the sun scorches them. Travel between the extremes.'

The wanderers of those oceans of bewildered unconscious have turquoise eyes,

So occasionally he glances up from pen and paper and peeps around that book,

What does he perceive, perhaps the shadow of a reaper who is a skeletal death?

Let us lobotomize those who cut so cruelly.

We can no longer tolerate the unholy Fool it is said

      but she's one latter-day saint,

Your lines of class and caste deceive no one but yourself the cunning bourgeois,

A simple cut in care is so deep a farrow ploughed by holy peasant strokes across

      that will be your sour Calvary,

The tilling of her arm, the cut through the skin will ring out with loud resonance in

YOUR CASH

REGISTER

Because we certainly have like the hunted turned hunters, yes you're now haunted.

The blade was drawn across an arm of pale flesh not a fallow field of financial notes

you had better start taking notes because yours are in tatters defaced and bankrupt,

A blade brings pain and blood you seem confused muddled now Capital is tumbling,

Let us lobotomize the reptiles that cut holy innocents with a scalpel, now they sweat.

He roams the catacombs at night with pen (2).

This dove with blood speckled on his beak beckons you bewildered vultures,

He is carrion on which you gorge your appetite for a feast of sacrificial writing,

The Lamb entombed in his mind with a pen and ink some paper without body,

Blessed is he amongst the lepers for they do suffer, no matter you can mutter,

Do you still worship all those hangings from that Tree of death, I ate the Apple

And know that maggots are burrowing out of my bulging eyes the sober Adam,

In gurgle of death a holy mother condemned both of us, Lamb and Magdalene.

Magdalene of illusion sits bemused and raving in her residence of a mad majesty,

I await death and scribe the words which echo around the catacombs of outcasts.

Cast the first stone preaches the priest.

Bourgeois understand the hands we priests swayed in praise were knurled twisted like

Bitter lemons floating in tumbler of vodka that was a draft of dark wine we drunk for you,

Nails were dug into plastic statues of a Christ by deranged middle-aged Pontius Pilates,

Not extracted by Magdalene or Hail Marys rushed off in a fever of rosary beads broken,

Cracked idols laugh loud deafening the pious and friends who are the cursed damned.

A stream of crystal nectar begins to trickle, gush a torrent like the necessity of History,

No the masses were only dormant, resurrected by revolutionaries conducting lighting,

A branding iron will burn a mark on the lily flesh of the dollar as Molotov cocktails blaze,

Not ethereal but delightfully physical women and men cast your stones, dawn is yours,

No judge but the vindication by humanity: 'the ends justify the means', Utopia on Earth.

Her Book of Cold Spells.

Moonbeams awake again as the White Goddess[2] has crackled into his mind like electricity,

This morning the pen scribbles because a poet's thighs are bound in tight bondage of blue,

A witch had locked the belt some barren desert drifting time ago with her brass prison key,

She peddled tears and fears from a pious silence, her book of charms only cast cold spells,

The bell had rung at birth to exorcize desire from her body that perished in pure purgatory,

Curses were cast in her casket; she gouged out hearts with a lunar crazed cardiac surgery.

---

[2] 'The White Goddess: a Historical Grammar of Poetic Myth' - Robert Graves (1948). Corrected, revised and enlarged editions appeared in 1952 and 1961. The White Goddess represents an approach to the study of mythology from a creative perspective. Graves argues the existence of a European Deity the "White Goddess of Birth, Love and Death" similar to the Mother Goddess inspired and represented by the phases of the Moon who lies behind the faces of the diverse goddesses of various European and pagan mythologies. Graves argues that "true" or "pure" poetry is inextricably linked with the ancient cult-ritual of his proposed White Goddess and of her son. These ideas influenced both Sylvia Plath and Ted Hughes.

To tickle love[3] again would not be metaphor, but a rook woman who writes with dark thread.

---

[3] 'If I was tickled by the rub of love' – Dylan Thomas (1934) [extract].

If I were tickled by the rub of love,
A rooking girl who stole me for her side...

I would not fear the apple nor the flood...
And that's the rub, the only rub that tickles.

And what's the rub? Death's feather on the nerve?
Your mouth, my love, the thistle in the kiss?...

I would be tickled by the rub that is:
Man be my metaphor.

Poem composed while contemplating the coming harvest by the masses. (b)

A harvest ready for History's reaper lies in the throes of death squirming and belching,

Scythes grasped by the oppressed like glistening steel catches the gold rays of dawn,

We have not forgotten the long dark nights of torment in homes, hospitals and prisons,

There are many dead, deformed dying and the waking dead victims already mummified,

Alive in bondage of bandages; but some patients brandish the bayonets of Bolshevism,

Have been hardened in the same foundries and factories as the swords of the masses,

They are of the furnace of that same collective eye, the many in One omniscient gaze

Glared before language could articulate agony the primal child spoke before aborted.

Us creatures are unbound Herr Dr Frankenstein, Prometheans who carry fiery plague,

An antidote to all mind numbing shackling medicines in your pharmacy, it is a revolution

To clear all that mind pollution of competitive evolution, the rats break free of your maze

Doc Skinner[4]: 'oh no they are misbehaving, revolting and breeding like 'Homo sapiens'.

Yes that is the rub of it the patients were not rats after all but are conscious proletarians,

The task to gather the crop of reactionaries and harvest it will not be like drama therapy.

---

[4] B. F. Skinner invented the operant conditioning chamber, popularly referred to as the Skinner Box to measure responses of organisms (often, rats and pigeons) and their ordered interactions with this environment. Skinner discovered that consequences on the organism played a large role in determining how the organism responded in these situations. For instance, when the rat would pull the lever it would receive food. He extrapolated from this his theory of Behaviorism in which human behavior is 'modified' by 'negative' or 'positive' reinforcement. Therefore Skinner believed introspection to be of no importance, psychology for Behaviorists is simply a question of the manipulation of human behavior by withdrawing or giving rewards

Nigel Pearce

The paper Buddhists.

The spectre is surrounded by shadows with their daggers drawn so do not exorcize.

Because of her

you are made flesh like all hermaphrodites her hungry Host prepares our salvation,

you dig the Beast[5]?

Your friends are on the mend man so why carry that sacrificial knife still unsheathed,

stop this inquisition, you like writing and do some chanting but we are still almost daft

drifting through webs of ideals not made of gossamer or metal structure of Mammon.

Turn of the screw[6] twist your blades.

---

[5] 'The beast that thou sawest was, and is not; and shall ascend out of the bottomless pit, and go into perdition: and they that dwell on the earth shall wonder, whose names were not written in the book of life from the foundation of the world, when they behold the beast that was, and is not, and yet is.'   - Revelation 17:8

[6] 'The Turn of the Screw.'- William James: 'One of the world's most famous ghost stories, the tale is told mostly through the journal of a governess and depicts her struggle to save her two young charges from the demonic influence of the eerie apparitions of two former servants in the household. The story inspired critical debate over the question of the "reality" of the ghosts and of James's intentions. James himself, in his preface to volume XII of The Novels and Tales of Henry James, called the tale a "fable" and said that he did not

Chalices of wine were like blood poured in ampules transmogrified into some caustic

Acid dripped mind, are you Holy Fool?[7]

We may be beached on isles, mirrors reflecting into each other, it is not stained glass

just shattered window panes.

Paper Buddhists cannot be unfolded as they were crumpled before they were born[8].

---

specify details of the ghosts' evil deeds because he wanted readers to supply their own vision of terror.'   The Merriam-Webster Encyclopaedia of Literature.

[7] 'One might well become a holy fool oneself here! It's catching!' Raskolnikov in Dostoevsky: 'Crime and Punishment'.

[8] Enlightenment as taught by Siddhartha Gautama known as the Buddha involves escape from the eternal cycle of rebirth called Samsara (literally in Sanskrit: 'wandering on.').

The poet hails a new generation of iconoclasts.

Stone stumps stand in disarray and spew their lies in twinkling twilight

these figurines are just like an imaginary harvest of grain in fallow land,

999 if you call 000 it is 666 chiselled onto their foreheads sad demons

impotent to resist the forces of these nights, they have no conscience

And will be gathered in a granary where a blind stone-mansion grinds,

resistance races through a poet's pen like his father's phallus, he had

Celebrated that patricide in a ceremony of self-immolation which was

SUBLIMATED

it became lines of snow drops on the child-poet's mind in the lunar light.

But wounds of lambs will no longer be cleaned with the antiseptic swabs, today's cuts are being dressed-up in gauze to avoid cross contamination.

Now those stone idols of yesterday crash, smashed by new generations of

ICONOCLASTS.

Nigel Pearce

The House of Ghosts.

He had recently regained his memory, the doctors had crammed him so full of tablets he'd burst. They had overmedicated, almost killed him. Noel was piecing together the jigsaw puzzle of those last 9 months. The chill of winter was still resonant in the winds, but the warmth of spring breezes crept in occasionally, it was a period of not one or the other. He had finally located Beech View House. It looked a rather large house and he wondered you got in, in seemed like a block of white-washed granite. No bell, but a metallic box with a button labelled 'press'. There was no reply, he pressed and pressed again, it must have been almost 15 minutes. What have they done to mum, this place? A short, rotund man of about 40 opened the door:

'Hello, my name is Noel, Mrs Price's son.'

'Yes, well…'

'Um, do you think I could see my mum? Unfortunately I haven't been able to visit because…'

'Mrs Price's son. Oh yes I remember being told about you.'

A wave of fear broke onto his wind swept beach. The tides had always caused the sands to shift at the best of times.

'…I'm her son Noel. I've been in hospital, sorry.' He stammered.

'So we've gathered.' The care-worked retorted sharply, it strike like a jab with a foil.

'St. James', it's a …'

'Loony bin.'

Noel tried to be firm: 'A psychiatric hospital and I was in the general one, both. '

'I'm not here to talk about your problems!'

'Sorry I just wanted to see mum. We're very close.'

'Very close, what do you mean?'

'What I say conveys its meaning in- itself, I would have thought.'

'Don't you think you should be standing on your feet, not bothering your elderly mother?'

'You misunderstand, I've come to visit her, have some real Turkish Delight from the bizarre, oh you know that specialist shop.'

'Bloody bizarre. Well come in, but we're about.'

There were people roaming along the corridors, some just bewildered, other muttering to themselves. They had lost what Sartre had called 'being-for-itself', nothingness drifting around in frail bodies. This place was indeed large, many houses knocked into one. He found Room 101, mum's room.

'Noel, thank God. You've come at last.'

'Mum, are you alright, what's been happening.'

'It is my younger sister; your aunt, she's had me put in here. Please take me away from this dreadful place.'

Noel gasped: 'You're not demented mum, I can tell. But I'm diagnosed with schizophrenia. I'm better with new medicine, but she's come down from up North, they don't know what's she's like. They will never believe us.'

'Son, it is a nightmare. She's ingratiated herself with the She's ingratiated herself with the doctor here. She went to the Court of Protection and had the Will changed, the doctor said I was incapable when I signed it.'

Noel thought quickly, the young aunt said there was a 'cool' doctor who was writing scripts for a gram of morphine a day. It all made sense now...

A modern psychomachy[9]

A troubled and largely sleepless night and Peter the priest scuttles like a frightened beetle out of his shell of reverie. His dreams are becoming a little too intense and seem to merge into wakefulness. The priest slumps beside the bed and prays:

'Holy Mother of God, the habit is returning, I beg you

Blessed Virgin, I've got to give it up'.

His skin is no longer young, not a fresh page on which to scribe poetry to the grandeur of God who had been his fountainhead in the early years. Alternatively it is not the wrinkled criss-crossed dried parchment of an old man awaiting his wake. His prayers seek solace in the Christ of the sacrament he celebrated at Mass daily.

'Jesus of the Holy Blood I need a hit of you like that first time I

celebrated the Holy Mass, what joy, unadulterated beauty. '

It had been over three years ago when he read Goethe aloud at an evening with some close priest friends from those spring sweet scented blossom seminar days. Father Liam had played a jig or two on his battered and scratchy violin. Those notes had pieced Peter's side like a knife and he had bled poetry:

'Two souls, alas, are housed within my breast,

and each will wrestle for the mastery there'.

---

[9] The term psychomachy comes from a Latin poem 'Psychomarcia' (c400BC) by Prudentitrus about the battle for a person's soul. In the Medieval period they were dramatized as 'morality plays.'

'Yes, Father Peter, Goethe again, very good and all well

when we were novices, but we're ordained priests.'

'I had noticed that Father Pious.'

'Come come, poetry and Father Pious' sherry.' smiled Father Liam.

He knew the others had looked-up to him in those days, but they were so staid except for Liam, not of the 'Kingdom of God'. But something snapped that night, a 'dark night of the soul' had engulfed Peter. His understanding of what was meant by the immaculate had been transformed; indeed body and soul were transmogrified almost like that quivering melody which caressed him from Liam's violin. Immaculate blood had meant only in the silver chalice he raised with extreme care to a line above his forehead for his meagre bunch of communicates to genuflect before. His parish had been mainly hypocrites and deceivers, a real bunch of Pharisees. One or two he had high hopes for like 'madman John':

No reason you cannot fulfil your vocation to the ideals of Saint Francis of Assisi.'

John had begun shoplifting and giving away stolen-goods to those street-addicts in the poor quarter. Yes that was a place for a priest to minister, but not to have their brown and white powders and those hellish off-white crystals administered to madman John or anyone else. He'd genuinely believed then the flock at Mass were different to those skeletal, emaciated creatures with taunt yellowing shin pulled around sunken eyes, those deep black hollows, those empty eyes, my God.

Peter quickly pulls on his baggy black priestly uniform which covers and gives some volume to a meagre frame, the rest he explains by his devotion to fasting. But then the cold burrows, almost bits, like a pulsating, squirming pile of purple worms and claws, eats into his body which would whiplash into some kind of sweat that seemed like a tropical fever. He knew that the mainline to the Divine is not the one recommended by his spiritual director, who he assiduously avoids, but the immaculate track which is marked by those stigmata which were nothing but regular neat lines of needle marks. Mass was at six fifteen, he needs to straighten-out for that, but he could not celebrate that Mass for those who attended so early where the real zealots and had the suspicions of your average drug-squad officer. What was the remedy? He knew only too well, it smashed through his skull into that tormented brain, of course there was nothing to worry about; he had stashed a little 'brown' away and with a couple or three tablets of diazepam he would be fit again, perhaps not to celebrate the Mass, but manage some kind of automated performance without his fingers becoming appendages of his hands fiddling feebly and trembling in a fumble out from his vestments.

He rummages under the sink, thank God, here's the stash. Unravel the brown paper in a flurry of hands, yes here's all that's required, praise be to whom, he wonders to God or to the 'man'? Suddenly Peter is disorientated no need to worry about 'madman John' he'll get through okay. Disengaging from the surroundings the priest thought he'd fall back into the tedium of the business at hand and it will be soon be Easter. Peter, with the precision of a locksmith, smoothed the silver paper, manoeuvres with the assistance of a razorblade a line of brown powder that within a minute or two will sooth the creases from his mind. The 'line' of brown powder is straight down the middle of the foil which he holds left handed. A cone had been inserted into his quivering lips, constructed of silver foil, lovingly three years ago. It is now fashioned by his claw like fingers into a utensil of pleasure no more than an instrument of necessity. In his right hand is an orange plastic lighter. He raises the left hand which holds the foil to within about four centimetres of the cone, ignites the lighter, a click, and with the swift yet careful movement of hand a flame scolds the silver foil; almost caressing it. The line of inanimate brown heroin bubbles into life, becomes suddenly a liquid then and finally, until the next time he 'chases the dragon', it becomes vapour. He inhales from right to left in one breath, then a pull from an already ignited cigarette...warmth engulfs his mind, then a womb-like peace enshrouds him. Finally he exhales stumbles and sits down.

'Not the mainline to the divine, but it will be adequate until later on.' Peter sighs aloud.

The tumbler of water is lifted, the three yellow tablets of diazepam swallowed.

'Give me half an hour and I'll be steady as the rock upon which the Church

is built.' He whispers playfully.

A series of waves which are like frenzied screeches resound through his mind: madman John

how are you, where are you, who are you? He is startled and gathers his paraphernalia

agitatedly, but with the paradox of addiction smoothly into the plastic bag which he places

and wraps in brown paper, then his stash is safe.

Mass then passed fairly uneventfully, a combination of him being 'comfortably numb' and the single track spirituality of the 6.15ers who knew the Mass so well it was less a ritual than a memorized piece of text which they'd pattered out for years, a sort of rapid mindless muttering. These acts of evasion; these deceptions were becoming more grotesque day by day he thought.

John, who had in many ways Peter pondered was the incarnation of the Franciscan ethic plus; plus what? The psychiatric nurses who would periodically whisk him into what remained of the local mental hospital, much of it lay derelict; care-in-the-community, seemed John didn't receive any 'meaningful' care, at best Peter would use the term management to describe it. What care did either of them really get, but chemical care? Then it hit him, he was beginning to withdraw. Had to get downtown and quickly to the market square and those familiar black clams of shame were beginning to attach themselves to his mind, would people realize he was going out to 'score'. The leeches of an unforgotten passion were sucking his moist flesh, he must forget:

Father, Father Peter, stop its John. I've been baptising near the river.

I'm John the Baptist.'

Holy shit thought the priest; he's really lost it this time and I need a hit.

Don't worry Father it's not full immersion, I'm 'doing them up' with pharmaceutical diamorphine.'

'Thank God.'

'It will soon be Easter Father, so I thought we'd better resurrect some of those downtown Lazarus people. St. Peter told me himself. You yourself Father Peter. '

'John you child, I'm not a saint, I'm a junkie.'

'We have the immaculate hit; I've got the ampoules here.'

'Perhaps there is something of Peter in me; I've denied my Master more than three times. There is no mainline to paradise John, we make that or not here on Earth and that is a dreadful burden, an awful freedom. John, let us drink deeply from the streams within our hearts.'

'What about the ampoules Father, why waste them.' John said.

A wry smile came over the gaunt face of the priest and exposed his yellow teeth:

'Well one for the road, just to say good-bye to it all.'

They were found with the blood congealing in their syringes. It was simple; they had forgotten to reduce the dosage for this was pharmaceutical heroin, not Lazarus gear and there would be no resurrection. Father Liam's violin had indeed played a drowsy melody to Peter, one that left him in the pleasure dome, but would with an irresistible and remorseless logic which left him a prisoner chained in the dark dungeons of addiction. Liam now has to hide the violin-case with fearful haste.

A 'fringe' performance of 'The Taming of The Shrew.'

My performance is set in Victorian London. This is because Ibsen's play *A Doll's House* was reviewed by Eleanor Marx at that time. It takes place in a theatre with proscenium arch and curtain. The audience sits in darkness, the antithesis of Early Modern theatre. In front of the curtain is a table and chairs. Behind is the interior of a bourgeois house of 1880's. Petruchio dressed as Helmer swaggers from the right Katherina dressed as Nora sits on a chair. A ragged dress lies on the table:

'O mercy God. What masking stuff is here?' 4.3.87.

Katherina is exhausted; she looks-up at her husband with fear. He holds the dress

'Why what a devil's name, tailor, call'st this?' 4.3.92

She backs away. The tailor enters from the left:

'You bid me make it orderly and well,

According to the fashion of the time.' 4.3. 94-95.

He smiles at Katherina:

'I never saw a better-fashioned gown.' 4.3.101.

They smirk at the well-dressed man.

The tailor says sarcastically:

'She says your worship wants to make a puppet of her.' 4.3.105.

Katharina mimics the actions of a doll pulled by strings and she and the tailor laugh.

Petruchio beside himself rages:

'O what monstrous arrogance!' 4.3.106.

He staggers forward and tears the dress:

Tailor laughs: 'Your worship is deceived. The gown is made

     'Just as my master had direction.'   4.3.114-115.

The curtain rises to show Hortensio and Grumio who had been enjoying one of his cigars. Grumio and the tailor fight a mock battle, Petruchio and Hortensio leave. The tailor and Grumio scamper into the wings on the left. The curtain falls leaving Katherina who lifts the hem of her dress to reveal a small brown bottle of laudanum held in her garter, she smiles:

From the wing the tailor:

'Why here is the note of fashion to testify,' 4.3.127.

Eleanor Marx stands-up in the audience saying 'drama is the opium of the people' and reads these words:

'Women are the creatures of an organized tyranny of men, as the workers are the creatures of an organized tyranny of idlers'

Eleanor Marx (1886) p.1.

She ascends the stage and embraces Christopher Sly.

Marx, E (1886) *The Women's Question from a Socialist Point of View*, London,

Thompson, A (ed) (2003 2nd edn) *The New Cambridge Shakespeare; The Taming of the Shrew*, Cambridge, Cambridge University Press.

Nigel Pearce

Two studies on Shakespeare: 'The Taming of the Shrew' and Romeo and Juliet.'

!) The Taming of The Shrew.

'The struggle in *The Shrew* is over possession of the word, as a

sign of power and status. The language of action, volition and

aggression is dominated in our usage by buried metaphor.'

Davies (1995) p 7.

Therefore I shall firstly argue that an analysis of language and secondly the fashion in which this language is portrayed in performance is central to understanding the patriarchal domination in this passage and the play. Scene IV is crucial to Petruchio's 'taming' of Katherina and her final demise. The passage begins with a taunting hyperbolic exclamation from Petruchio:

'O mercy God!' (4.3.87)

This is followed by a series of puns: 'Marry' (4.3.96), 'mar' (4.3.97) and 'marred' (4.3.115) on their marriage. Thompson identifies this 'pun' on marriage as 'ruin in the following fashion with the pun on marry' (4.3.96n). Also present is the alliterative repetition of 'm' sounds which together with 'masking' (4.3.87) almost mocks the marriage. It is a method of laughing at the 'other':

'We might call it Hobbesian after Thomas Hobbes who defined laughter as an 'expression of superiority."

Berry (2002) p.123.

The 'others' are Katherina and the 'tailor':

'Ladies' tailors were comic figures on early modern stage –

characters whose masculinity was bought into question.'

Kidnie (2006) p.74.

The tailor employs two iambic pentameters (4.3.94/95), which after further ridicule from Petruchio, Katherina answers with an iambic pentameter, the first of the only three lines of her's in the passage:

'I never saw a better fashioned gown.' (4.3. 101)

These lines create a sense of ordered solidarity between the 'others'.

The affinity between 'others' is maintained with the same imagery being employed by Petruchio to describe the tailor as he had earlier to Katherina, that of 'devil.' See (1.1.66) (1.1.88) and (11.1.26) in relation to Katherina:

Petruchio: 'Why, what a devil's named, tailor, call'st thou this?' (4.3.92)

Hortensio in an aside confirms the misogyny. She has been deprived of food and sleep, now the clothes she likes:

Hortensio [Aside] 'I see she's like to have neither cap nor gown.' (4.3.93)

With the stress on 'cap' and 'gown's the metre has been disrupted to draw the audience's attention to this. The use of simile of comparing the fitting for the gown to an 'apple-tart' (4.3.89) is used to compound the cruelty of her deprivation of food. Thompson identifies 'apple-tart'

(4.3.89) as 'deliberately tantalise Katherina with thoughts of food' (4.3.89n).

A metaphor of a puppet, a plaything (Thompson 4.4.103 identifies 'puppet with doll, plaything 4.4.103n), is emphasised by rhyme between the two main characters:

Katherina: 'Belike you mean to make a puppet of me.' (4.3.103)

    Petruchio: 'Why, true, he means to make a puppet of thee.' (4.3.104)

But here is an example another aspect Petruchio's 'taming' scheme, deception, for it is he not the tailor (which is implied) who is making a 'puppet' of Katherina.

 Petruchio: 'Here's snip and nip and cut and slish and slash.' (4.3.90)

This is an example of:

'His pathological violent verbal and physical behaviour upon which the patriarchal system of marriage, the subordination of women and the ownership of property are founded.'

Davis (1995) p 6.

We can hear the relentless threatening iambs, the force of the internal rhyme 'snip' and 'nip' followed by 'cut' and the violent onomatopoeia of 'slish and slash'. This is not 'farce' it is oppression and domination. There is no irony here.

Stichomythia is employed between Grumio and the tailor between 4.3.17-4.3.22, this creates a sense of rapid fire exchanges which culminates in the ambiguous:

Grumio: 'Face not me. Thou hast braved many men; brave not me. I will neither be faced nor braved.' 4.3. (123-124)

Grumio uses prose as opposed to the blank verse of the bourgeois characters. As McEvoy argues (see McEvoy (2000) pp. 18-20) different 'registers of language' are used to create characterisation, in this instance the contrast of prose and poetry reflects differences in social class.

Bibliography.

BBC Television Shakespeare: *The Taming of the Shrew*, 1980.

Berry, E (2002) *Laughing at "others"* in Leggart, A (ed) The Cambridge Companion to Shakespearean Comedy, Cambridge, Cambridge University Press.

Berry, R (1988) *Shakespeare and Social Class*, New Jersey, Humanities Press International.

Davies, S (1995) *The Taming of The Shrew*, London, Penguin Critical Studies.

Kidnie, M (2006) *The Taming of the Shrew: a guide to the text and its theatrical life*, Palgrave Macmillan.

Leggart, A,(ed) (2002) *The Cambridge Companion to Shakespearian Comedy*, Cambridge, Cambridge University Press.

Marx, E (1886) *The Women's Question from a Socialist Point of View*, London, Westminster Review.

McEvoy, S (2000) *Shakespeare: the basics*, London, Routledge.

Pacheco, A. (ed) *Shakespeare* A177 Study Guide, Milton Keynes, The Open University.

Schafer, E (2002) *The Taming of the Shrew: Shakespeare in Production*, Cambridge, Cambridge University Press.

Thompson, A (ed) (2003 2nd edn) *The New Cambridge Shakespeare; The Taming of the Shrew*, Cambridge, Cambridge University Press.

Warren, R (2005) *The Taming of the Shrew*, York Notes Advanced, London, York Press.

'

Romeo and Juliet

In order to reappraise Shakespeare's play it is necessary to construct an analysis which examines whether the feud between the two families and the ideology which surrounds it determines a tragic conclusion to the play and this in turn requires an evaluation of the nature of ideology and tragedy in relation to the feud. I shall explore both macro-historical analysis and micro-historical explanations of these central questions. Beginning with a definition of ideology located in Marx which informs the methodology I have favoured:

'The sum total of the relations of production constitutes the economic structure of society, the real foundation, upon which rises a legal and political superstructure which correspond definite forms of social consciousness.'

Marx, *Selected Works* (2007) p 425.

Therefore the superstructure or ideology which includes literature is a 'reflex', in the last instant, of the economic base. Ideas and literature do not, I would argue, have universal forms which transcend the conditions of production. However ideology is not neutral and serves an objective social function as Terry Eagleton has maintained:

'The function of ideology is to legitimise the power of the ruling class; in the last analysis the dominant ideas of a society are those of its ruling class.'

Eagleton, *Marxism and Literary Criticism* (1976) p 5.

My central thesis is that the feud is the engine of the play. It is this that transforms *Romeo and Juliet* from a 'tragedy of character' to being a 'tragedy of situation'; the latter allows for a socio-economic dimension. In this process it is clear how Shakespeare transcends Aristotle's definition of tragedy in *Poetics,* Hutton (1982). Here Aristotle required three elements: firstly *hamartia* or 'tragic flaw' or more accurately mistaken action, secondly the protagonist's *peripeteia* or change for the worse and thirdly their *anagnorisis* or 'realization' of the true state of things. In Romeo and Juliet Shakespeare reinvents Aristotle's theory of tragedy making his play a product of the objective material conditions in which he lived; emergent patriarchal capitalism rather than innate character traits. Shakespeare has used Brooke's source material, reinvented it in the context of his epoch and created a new poetics which is a critique of the society in which he lived. His play illustrates the contradictions of that society i.e. warring noble families, the shock of new property forms as the 'primitive accumulation of capital' took place and the Bonapatist nature of the regime/state inherent in the Prince who reflects the new state struggling to control the warring families. The differentiation of Romeo and Juliet from the epoch's dominant ideology of patriarchal capitalism is central to the feud within the play and to my argument. This thesis is derived from the historical materialist methodology outlined above and it will be illustrated by both primary and secondary sources.

'Two households, both alike in dignity In fair Verona, where we lay our scene.

Shakespeare (2000), Prologue 1-2.

The Chorus here presents a material and class analysis of the plot and as Berry (1988) p 38 points out 'socially there is nothing to choose between the Montagues and the Capulets; two distinguished and well-founded families'. The feud mentioned in Prologue 3-4 is characterised by an ideology of patriarchal violence with constant references to swords and daggers welded by men in the public sphere which in patriarchal capitalism is the masculine arena. The epoch of the 'primitive accumulation of capital':

'In the history of primitive accumulation, all revolutions are epoch-making that act as levers for the capital class in course of formation; but, above all, those moments when great masses of men are suddenly and forcibly torn from their means of subsistence, and hurled as free and "unattached" proletarians on the labour market. In England alone, which we take as our example, has it the classic form. '

Marx, (2007) p532

This is a transition phase between the feudal and capitalist modes and is therefore unstable; Shakespeare reflects this in the feud and the rebellion of the lovers against patriarchal bonds. Juliet in the motor of the rebellion a) she proposes marriage and also challenges the 'honour culture' but it is veiled as she doesn't know Romeo is listening. Her emotions are 'authentic' they do not depend on the 'gaze' of the male 'subject'; she defies patriarchy by refusing to allow her love to be the 'object' of Romeo:

'Deny thy father and refuse thy name;

Or if thou not, be sworn my love,

And I'll no longer be a Capulet.'

Shakespeare (2000) 2.1.77-79.

and b) she creates a metamorphosis in Romeo who renounces that ideology paradoxically as he revenges it:

Nigel Pearce

'O sweet Juliet

Thy beauty has made me effeminate.'

Shakespeare (2000) 3.1 113-114.

For: 'All that is solid melts into air' Marx (2007) p248.

Their love is subversive and their suicide, which Camus (1976) argues is the only philosophical problem is equally revolutionary because of the 'silence'. The Elizabethan audience would have believed suicide to be a 'mortal sin' and it is therefore fetishized. Montague then wants to build a:

'...statue of pure gold.'

Shakespeare (2000) 5.3 299.

Of Juliet, but this is the fetishism of the cash nexus, the nascent 'exchange-value' of commodity capitalism:

'There is a physical relation between physical things. But it is different with commodities. .... There it is a definite social relation between men, that assumes ... the fantastic form of a relation between things. In [the religious] world the productions of the human brain appear as independent beings endowed with life, and entering into relation both with one another and the human race. So it is in the world of commodities with the products of men's hands. This I call the Fetishism.'

Marx (2007) p473-4.

Therefore the only way the mechanism of historical necessity can control them is to turn them into golden idols/phalluses. This is not a tragedy of 'flawed characters' but one created by and driven by the contradictions of the epoch it was written in, it is determined by social being.

.   From a different perspective Julia Kristeva in *'Romeo and Juliet: Love-Hatred in the Couple* (1985) made an important contribution to understanding of the 'inner' forces within the feud that drives the tragedy. She does not argue that *hamartia* or Divine predestination determines the tragedy, but unconscious forces located within the lovers heightened by the patriarchal ideology of the feud that must inevitably destroy their idealized love. She suggests that Romeo and Juliet's love is defined in opposition to the feud which is embedded in the families. It is therefore inevitably a 'transgressive love, outsider love' (ibid) for they live in fear of the feuding families who are like social manifestations of a Freudian 'Superego' or parental conscious. She argues that the lover, particularly the woman lover, desires her love to be within the law which in psychoanalytical terms means to merge with the Ego Ideal.

'So it is no accident that both Romeo and Juliet fall for another member of a family they have been socialized to hate.'

Harris, *Shakespeare and Literary Theory* (2010) p 100-101

This is seen as an unconscious drive. Kristeva deconstructs and complexifies her argument further for although their love defies patriarchy it also contains the paradox that within Juliet, the feminine:

'My only love sprung from my only hate.'

Shakespeare (2000) 1.4.251.

So there is the contradiction of love and hate as Kristeva (1985) explains:

'What is involved is hatred at the very origin of this amorous stage.'

White (ed) *Romeo and Juliet: Contemporary Critical Essays* (2001) p34

Their love is doomed because it is an adolescent 'idealized' Oedipal complex and therefore vulnerable to violent emotions which the feud exacerbates. She concludes that if the Romeo and Juliet had managed to extricate themselves from the feud and its complications they would have gone on to live 'a banal, humdrum' existence or 'a life of sadomasochism' (Kristeva 1987, 217). For Kristeva then this idealized youthful love cannot escape the feud and its ideology. Eros and the grinding nature of patriarchal law are antithetical as Friar Lawrence states:

'She's not well married that lives married long,

But she's best married that dies married young.'

Shakespeare (2000) 4.5. 77-8.

I would argue that her analysis is persuasive within the confines of psychoanalytic criticism, but it merely serves to 'pathologise' the protagonists and reduces the question of tragedy in relation to the feud to psychological determinism, located not in the stars or society but in the unconscious.

In conclusion I have examined Marxian and a psychoanalytical perspective of the play and concluded it is a tragedy fuelled by the feud. However I have suggested the Shakespeare contravenes the laws of Aristotle *Poetics* in regard of tragedy and rather sees a determined model either in society or the unconscious. Finally I would argue that what makes this 'tragedy of love' so poignant is its ability to subvert the dominant ideology of its epoch, but also what makes Shakespeare a great writer is his ability to reflect the contradictions of the early modern period, Christopher Caudwell (1937) p 64-5 commented correctly and to a large extent encapsulates my view:

'Shakespeare could not have attained the stature he did if he had not exposed, at the dawn of bourgeois development, the whole movement of capitalist contradiction.'

Bibliography.

Berry, R (1988) *Shakespeare and Social Class,* Humanities Press International, N.J.

Baldick, C (2008) *The Oxford Dictionary of Literary Terms*, Oxford University Press.

Callaghan, D. Helms, L. Singh, J (1994) *The Weyward Sisters,* Blackwell.

Camus, A (1976) *The Myth of Sisyphus,* Penguin Modern Classics.

Caudwell, C (1937) *Illusion and Reality: a study in the sources of poetry*, People's Publishing House, Bombay.

Chedgzoy, K (ed) (2001) *Shakespeare, Feminism and Gender; Contemporary Critical Essays*, Palgrave Macmillan

Dustinberre, J (2003) *Shakespeare and the Nature of Woman*, Palgrave Macmillan.

Dutton, R. Howard J (eds) (2006) *A Companion to Shakespeare's Works, Volume 1 The Tragedies,* Blackwell Publishing.

Eagleton, T (1976) *Marxism and Literary Theory*, Routledge.

Egan, G (2004) *Shakespeare and Marx*, Oxford University Press.

Freud, S (1995) (ed) Gay, P *The Freud Reader*, London, Vintage Books.

Harris, J.G. (2010) *Shakespeare and Literary Theory*, Oxford University Press.

Hutton, J (trans) Aristotle *Poetics*, New York, Norton.

Kristeva, J (1985) *Romeo and Juliet: Love-Hate in the Couple* in White, R.S (ed) (2001) Romeo and Juliet: Contemporary Critical Essays, Palgrave Macmillan

Kristeva, J (1987) *Tales of Love* in Harris (2010) Shakespeare and Literary Theory. Oxford University Press.

Marx (2007) McLellan, D (ed) *Selected Writings*, Oxford University Press

McEachern, C (ed) (2011) *A Cambridge Guide to Shakespearian Tragedy*, Cambridge University Press.

Shakespeare, W (2000) (ed) Levenson *Romeo and Juliet* The Oxford Shakespeare, Oxford University Press.

White, R.S (ed) (2001) *Romeo and Juliet; Contemporary Critical Essays*, Palgrave Macmillan

Writing for today: Aesthetics and Critical Theory.

The surrealist poet and writer Andre Breton stated:

'To reduce imagination to slavery...even if one's so-called

happiness is at stake – means to violate all that one finds

in one's inmost self of ultimate justice.

Imagination alone tells me what can be.'.[10]

A leading member of The Frankfurt School which developed 'Critical Theory' argued:

'Art and so-called classical art no less than it's more

anarchical expressions, always was and is, a force of

protest of the humane against the pressure of domineering

institutions, religions and otherwise, no less than it reflects

their objective substance.'[11]

Herbert Marcuse would write of this artistic 'Great Refusal' in the context of Surrealism,

Freud and that of Critical Theory that it was a protest against 'unnecessary repression'

(Marcuse: Eros and Civilisation, p.149). But today as the world is convulsed by what could be the 'death-throes' of capitalism what is the way ahead for writers and artists, certainly it is in the vanguard of the masses but as Lenin had argued in *What Is To Be Done?* quite

---

[10] Manifestes du Surrealisme. (1924) [1946] p 15 Paris: Editions du Sagittaire

[11] Adorno (1945) Thesis on Art and Religion Today Kenyon Review

VII. 4, p 678.

some time before the initially successful workers insurrection of October 1917 in Russia:

'There can be no revolutionary activity without revolutionary theory.'[12]

We can look to 'The Frankfurt School' for some answers to these questions with their fusion of Marxism, psychoanalysis and existential philosophy which they applied to the whole spectrum of thought; here we will examine what they can tell writers and artists in the context of aesthetics. We will see how significant the writings of the young Marx, Freud and Lukács were for these writers and how they developed in response to the struggles of the oppressed from 1917 to the present day with their unique ideas about writing, music and art. They analysed not only the contemporary writers who formed Modernism like Kafka and Samuel Beckett, but also writers such as Baudelaire who had created, in response to shifting material conditions, the foundations of modern writing. Particularly I shall investigate the concepts regarding modernity and the nature of the poet and aesthetics in Walter Benjamin and particularly his debate with Theodor Adorno over this question and finally reject subsitutionalism.

The group had its roots in the wave of revolutions which sweep Europe in 1917-1922 and particularly the October revolution in Russia and the workers revolts in Germany and Italy. These events would change qualitatively the aspirations of the international proletariat and their historical direction and transform the intellectual world, the reverberations of these events and ideas can be felt in the mass anti-capitalist movements of today. However the world of writing and art would also experience concomitant creative

---

[12] Lenin, What Is To Be Done? 1902, CW, Vol.5, p.369. Progress Publishers, Moscow

pulsations emanating from these mass revolutionary waves. These revolutions put Marxism firmly on the agenda of the proletariat who were fulfilling what Engels had argued was their 'world historic mission', but also for the intelligentsia and the avant-garde in literature, art and music. Only those paralysed by the class interests of the bourgeois could try and ignore it and they would be influenced by these earthquakes because they were its dialectical opposite, its antithesis.

This school of communists were not Stalinists, Maoists nor really in the Trotskyist

tradition, but 'dissident Marxists' who were inspired by those early heady days of working class revolution and applied rigor and innovatory analysis to the questions of literature, art and music, They were Neo-Marxist intellectuals and founded 'The Institute of Social Research' or as it became known as 'The Frankfurt School' in 1923. The term 'Critical Theory' only came into usage in 1937 once they had fled Nazi Germany for America. They are associated with ideas of 'alienation', 'reification' and notably for the purposes of this article their ground-breaking examination of aesthetics. They numbered amongst their grouping and those closely associated with it some of the most significant thinkers of modern times: Max Horkheimer, Theodor W. Adorno, Herbert Marcuse, Erich Fromm, Walter Benjamin, and Jürgen Habermas.

The Frankfurt School would find much intellectual material in *The Philosophical and*

Economic Manuscripts[13] of Marx which were not published until 1930, the ideas of Sigmund Freud and of the Hungarian Marxist Georg Lukács; paradoxically many of those who identify with Lukács perceive the Frankfurt School as deviationists from Marxist tradition. As I shall show these are contentious issues within the communist and revolutionary socialist traditions. Many Marxists would claim that The Frankfurt School's analysis was revisionist and the German communist dramatist and poet Bertolt Brecht would enter into fierce denunciations of some of their positions as do Trotskyists and other Leninists. The followers of the variant of Neo-Marxism propagated by Louis Althusser are also critical of them. However detached from the class struggle they appear they have some important contributions and insights which fellow Marxists should consider in a comradely fashion.

Withstanding that Lukács' great work of 1923, *History and Class Consciousness* was

particularly important to the Frankfurt School:

'Let us assume for the sake of argument that recent research had disproved once and for all every one of Marx's individual thesis. Even if this were to be proved, every serious 'orthodox' Marxist would still be able to accept all such modern findings without reservations...orthodox Marxism does not imply the uncritical acceptance of the results of Marx's investigation. It is not the 'belief' in this or that thesis nor the exegesis of a 'sacred' book. On the contrary,

---

[13] Marx (1844) [2007] Selected Works, ed. David MacLellan, p 83-122 Oxford University Press.

orthodoxy refers exclusively to method.'[14]

This was a profound insight by Lukács but was no more than Marx himself had suggested when he said 'I am not a Marxist'. However it freed the Frankfurt School from the bondage of any form of text literalism, those chains of a sacred text chiselled in stone and gave them a methodology which could be used to incorporate and revisit previous texts, this is the beauty of this group of Marxist thinkers. It lead to huge gains in terms of theoretical innovation but also lead to them transcending the method they began with. So with the others who undertook what Herbert Marcuse had called the Great Refusal [Denial] which is mentioned in *Inferno* Canto 3 as the antechamber of Hell, it is the place of prevarication:

'Those who made the Great Denial.

At once I understood for certain: these

were of that retrograde and faithless crew'[15]

Dante6.

Of course the 'Great Denial' mentioned in Dante is to serve neither God nor 'his enemy'.

This is mirrored in the epoch of 'moribund capitalism' (Lenin) in which humanity had already

experienced the 'Death of God' in the 19th century as articulated by Friedrich Nietzsche:

'God is dead! God remains dead! And we have killed him.

---

[14] Lukács (1923) History and Class Consciousness in Bronner

(2011) Critical Theory p.21, Oxford

[15] Dante (1308-1321) [1900] Inferno: Canto iii line 57-60, Temple Press.

How shall we comfort ourselves, the murderers of all murderers? What was holiest and mightiest of all that the world has yet owned has bled to death under our knives: who will wipe this blood off us? What water is there for us to clean ourselves? What festivals of atonement, what sacred games shall we have to invent? Is not the greatness of this deed too great for us? Must we ourselves not become gods simply to appear worthy of it?'[16]

- Nietzsche7,

So today the class struggle is not projected into the religious realm, today we are confronted by the choice between the two major contending classes of our epoch: the proletariat or its enemy the decadent bourgeoisie? One cannot sit on the fence as the contradictions inherent in capitalism hurl it into the abyss. It is clear that at the genesis of the Frankfurt School they were absolutely clear about this, but may have chased their own tail into a circle leading back to its beginning; theory without practice and the consequent theoretical errors of this process. This represented a failure to understand the nature of 'praxis' as delineated by Sartre. However before any descent in meaningless exegesis there was much sharp analysis. This is what I shall now describe in relation to literature and art and will argue that these *ideas themselves become weapons in the hands of writers*. But those ideas alone cannot substitute for the activity of the masses in transforming society

To encapsulate and expand on the material basis of the Frankfurt School and Critical

Theory it is possible to suggest that they were born in the furnace of working class

---

[16] Nietzsche (1882) [1956] The Gay Science section 125, Meridian Books

revolution, but then when in 1929 economic crisis shock capitalism to its foundations some elements within the masses turned to fascism rather than socialism for a solution. The metanarrative of the Frankfurt School's very existence was challenged. They had understood from Lukács that 'method is orthodoxy' for Marxists and they incorporated the work of Sigmund Freud into their ideas. Why? Because according to Marxist understanding proletarian 'class consciousness' should have risen from 'trade union consciousness' to 'revolutionary consciousness' in this period, it didn't. So one looks to the unknown, the recently discovered realms of the unconscious of psychoanalysis:

'The unconscious is the larger circle which includes within itself the smaller circle of the conscious; everything conscious has its preliminary step in the unconscious, whereas the unconscious may stop with this step and still claim full value as a psychic activity. Properly speaking, the unconscious is the real psychic; it's inner nature is just as unknown to us as the reality of the external world.' Freud[17][18]

Hence following Freud the conscious needs of the proletariat were 'repressed' by institutions such as the family. Engels (1884) *The Origins of The Family, Private Property and The State*) argued that the family group as a unit as opposed to the kinship group in a communal setting was an instrument of oppression and Wilhelm Reich (1929*) Historical Materialism and Psychoanalysis* incorporated Freud's ideas into this position. It is here that we can perceive the influence of psychoanalysis, but also the reason why it was

---

[17] Freud (1920) Dream Psychology

[18]

http://en.wikipedia.org/w/index.php?title=Psychoanalysis&oldid=4601 75229 necessary, for this grouping, to introduce Freud into the Marxist current. Once this was done and the revolutionary communist movement was in retreat in the West and being betrayed by the Stalinist falsifiers in the USSR, Trotsky (1935) *The Revolution Betrayed*, anything was possible in the realm of theory.

Hence Walter Benjamin was therefore analysing literature in this context and arguing that:

'There is no document of civilization which is not at the

same time a document of barbarians.'

- Walter Benjamin[19]

However his theory of art was peculiar to him and was out of step with the mainstream of the Frankfurt School's position on artistic matters. He begins with the concept of 'automatous art' which has an 'aura' which is unique within the group. For him, art began to serve ritualistic cults. Therefore art was embedded in ritual and tradition, argues Benjamin, and has this 'aura', a specialness you could say. It is authenticated by magical tradition, it has a 'semblance of autonomy' and as long as poetry and art was in that tradition it retain its 'unique existence', this 'aura'. But Benjamin argues once the age of mechanical reproduction i.e. capitalism came into existence the private and ritualistic nature of art was lost; in other words it lost 'autonomy'. This process for Benjamin occurred 'unconsciously and once it has occurred the nature and purpose of art is radically altered. He wrote in *The work of art in the age of mechanical reproduction* (1936)

'The instant the criterion of authenticity ceases to be

applicable to artistic production, the total function of

art is reversed. Instead of being based on ritual, it

---

[19] Walter Benjamin in Jay (1996) The Dialectical Imagination p 173, University of California Press.

begins to be based on another practice – politics'[20]

Although this represented a 'sense of loss' (ibid) it was a victory both for writers and readers because it could potentially bring the masses in closer proximity to literature and culture. And here is the writer and artist gains the potential for emancipation:

'Mechanical reproduction emancipates the work of art from its parasitical dependence on ritual.'

    - ibid.

Here, I would suggest in modernity although the artist may be alienated from ritual s/he

therefore becomes desacralized, becomes truly human. Walter Benjamin's view of mass culture, unlike Adorno and Horkheimer, was positive in this context. This is a major contribution to modern thinking as the potential for the 'aura', the mysticism of writing and art can be stripped away and for it to achieve fruition in the material base which is the human subject in all its complexities both conscious and unconscious. This cannot be achieved under capitalism, although that has revolutionized the 'means of production' and therefore 'artist production' it still fetters these by the nature of private ownership. Brecht was a friend of Benjamin and sympathetic to his ideas.

Adorno conversely reacted adversely to Benjamin's ideas on writing in a letter claiming he did not understand Marxist dialectics;

'If one wants to speak drastically, one could say the work

settled in a crossroads between magic and positivism. This

spot is bewitched. Only theory can break the spell.'[21]

---

[20] The work of art in the age of mechanical production' in Illuminations (1968), p 224, Fontana Books.

[21] Adorno quoted in Jay (1996) The Dialectical Imagination p, 208. University of California Press.

Benjamin replied with haste:

'The appearance of a closed factuality, which adheres to philological investigation and casts a spell on the researcher, will disappear to the extent that the object will be constructed in historical perspective. The base lines of this construction converge in our own historical experience.'[22]

The tensions between the two men are evident as well as the theoretical differences and the essay was published independently of the Institute, but it is as a prelude to further development by both thinkers into aesthetics that interests us here. Benjamin and Adorno shared an awareness of the erosion of aesthetic traditions with the development of 'mass culture'. This genuine cultural experience or *Erfahrungen* seemed to be eroded in the capitalism of the 1930's, certainly by fascism. Benjamin saw an example in his study on Baudelaire in which he describes the 'crowd', often referenced in the work of the Frankfurt School on Mass Culture and therefore significant to the comprehension of their ideas regarding aesthetics and writing in the modern world, Benjamin writes:

'Baudelaire saw fit to equate the men of the crowd with the flâneur (idler). I find it hard to accept this view.'

- ibid

The other members of the institute feared not so much was the erosion of traditional art but the consequences of that in the historical circumstances; it's being opposed by a

diametrically fascist opposite one. Here Benjamin supported Brecht who saw a new

---

[22] The work of art in the age of mechanical production' in Illuminations (1968), p 224, Fontana Books.

communist future in the 'new'. However I would maintain that this was an early manifestation of an inherent ideological conservatism in Adorno and Horkheimer which had its roots in a misinterpretation of the nature of the 1930's which was remedied by Trotsky (1938) *The Death Agony of Capitalism and The Tasks of the Fourth International.*[23]15 This conservatism would later be manifest in Adorno in his writing on the 'counter-culture' and with Horkheimer the degeneration of their commitment to the instrumental role of the working class in social transformation.

What lessons can writers and artists draw from this debate as we spiral into a Recession in many ways similar to that of the 1930's? We should follow Lukács and see 'method as orthodoxy', we should embrace the new in aesthetics, renounce elitist ideas about the role of

writers and artists and finally remember Marx said: 'That the emancipation of the working classes must be conquered by the working classes themselves'16 and not attempt to substitute any group for that 'class'.[24]

---

[23] www.marxists,org/archive/trotsky/1938/tp/index.htm

[24] Marx (1864) [1981] The First international and after, p 83 Penguin Books

Mass Strike: theory and practice.

'The mass strike has now become the centre of lively interest of the international working class because it is a new form of struggle.'[25]

As the global recession bits and provokes a response in the proletariat and their allies, the oppressed, we have seen 2011/12 become the year of revolutions, across the globe there have been revolutions and mass strikes.

Therefore the question of the theory, practice and history of the Mass Strike in its relationship to transitional demands and maximalist demand of revolution is of great interest to all class-conscious workers today. How have the material conditions been created which objectively compels the proletariat to fight upon the stage of History, once again, arisen:

'Two decades of US global hegemony has brought the world to the deepest and most destructive economic crisis since the Second World War. First the credit system was paralysed. Then world trade and production slumped. Panicked by the prospect of complete economic meltdown, the leaders of the most powerful nations agreed to huge state bailouts of bankrupt banks that were deemed too big to fail, and launched massive stimulus packages to avoid the collapse of capitalism. From the acolytes of Milton Friedman to the apostles of John Maynard Keynes, the response was the same – spend billions,

---

[25] Luxemburg, Rosa. (1906) The Mass Strike, the Political Party and the Trade Unions.

trillions, to rescue the system..and recoup the losses later. This "sovereign debt crisis" has crystallised into a series of huge austerity programmes as the ruling class tries to make the working class pay for the crisis through public sector job losses, tax increases, wages and pension freezes and savage cuts in welfare provision. The credit crunch, recession and debt time–bomb of 2008–2012 opened a new historic crisis for the capitalist system as a whole, a period in such intense struggles between the classes will give rise to revolutionary crises and counter–revolutions. This is not just a typical downswing of the industrial cycle, one of the 'ordinary' ups and downs of the system. Its roots lie in the system's tendency to the over–accumulation of capital. In the period ahead, the overall curve of humanity's development will be downward until either the capitalists inflict a huge defeat on the working class around the world, laying waste to productive capacity and plunging millions into poverty or capitalism is itself overthrown.'[26]

It is of crucial importance for us understand the nature of the Mass Strike as theorised, particularly, through them writings of Karl Marx, Engels, Rosa Luxemburg and Leon Trotsky. This in turn allows us to comprehend the errors of on one hand the Marxian Centrist vacillators and Syndicalists and the Reformists on the other.

Marx argued:

'The emancipation of the working class is the act of the working class.'[27]

And that therefore it is the proletariat who create themselves as historical agents and because of that the theory of the working class

---

[26] 'From Resistance to Revolution': Programme of the League for a 5th International (2011).

[27] Marx, K (1998) Selected Works.

is the product of the struggle of the oppressed rather than existing in some abstract sphere detached from the daily experiences of women and men.

The first General Strike took place in Scotland in 1820 in response to the infamous Peterloo massacre and the continuing government repression. In January of that year they decided:

'That there should be a Strike of work everywhere to continue for some days to effectuate an insurrection.'[28]

Unfortunately the Glasgow workers were unable to spread or 'generalize' their activity and the strike was smashed. However the concept of a Mass Strike which would lead to a revolution had been introduced into the history of working-class and this was a 'qualitative leap' in proletarian consciousness. In 1832 a radical cobbler called William Benbow, who was on the 'Left' of the Chartists Movement in England argued that the masses lacked:

'A knowledge of ourselves; a knowledge of our own power, of our immense might, and the right we have to employ in action that immense power.'[29]

.

By 1842 a massive revolutionary General Strike was taking place which involved 500,000 workers, but lacking a coherent revolutionary programme it declined into defeat. These two events affected both Marx and Engels learning the lessons and they argued from 1851 that the proletariat must smash the state-machine:

'Every revolution overthrows the existing state, to this extent, it is political'[30].

---

[28] M Thomis and P Holt (1977) Threats of Revolution in Britain 1798-1848.

[29] Benbow, W in Crook, W. H (1960) Communism and the General Strike.

And as importantly Engels, speaking at the First International maintained that is was vital that there was a fusion of the economic and political struggles, hence:

'Workers should no allow separation of their economic movement from their political activity'[31]

These would become the keys to the problem of the mass strike which later become finely polished by Rosa Luxemburg and Leon Trotsky and we shall see how they were applied to conditions of mass working class activity during the last thirty years.

Luxemburg's key document: 'The Mass Strike' was her analysis of the wave of mass strikes which swept Belgium, Germany, Poland and culminated in the failed 1905 revolution in Russia. Rosa had been an active revolutionary socialist in a right-ward moving organization, the SDP, in Germany and she had engaged the revisionist leadership in open debate, but at this time remained in the organization. A wave of grass-root strikes hit Belgium on May 1st 1891 with 125,000 workers taking action, although the strike failed in its immediate demand, the right to vote, it made an impact on the leadership of the reformist workers party. They then used the tactic in 1893 and called a General Strike and won significant if limited concessions. This put the whole idea of the General Strike back on the agenda of the Second International. The SDP was the largest section within the International and debate between the three main factions was intensified: 1) the 'don't rock the boat' leadership,

---

[30] Marx, K (1927) Collected Works

[31] Engels, F (1870) Resolutions of the London Delegate Conference; International Working Man's Association.

2) a 'centrist' grouping lead by the revisionist Kautsky and 3) 'left' revolutionary faction lead by Rosa Luxemburg.

All three groupings were engaged in a debate lead by the reactionary Bernstein who argued for a 'gradualist' approach encapsulated in his now infamous remark that 'the movement was everything and in comparison socialism was nothing', think you will recognise that 'sell-out' resounding in the British Labour Party over the years. The rightist leadership backed him totally, but Kautsky took a slightly more subtle 'line' arguing that a General Strike could be revolutionary, but only if controlled by the leadership which is sometimes called 'the bureaucracy'. Although Lenin disagreed with Kautsky over many questions the Russian revolution of October 1917 eventually 'degenerated' (Trotsky) 'distorting' a genuine workers revolution. As Lenin stated in 1919, we are living in a 'bureaucratically distorted workers state'. However the 'left' faction within the SPD and its theoretician

Luxemburg had been more profoundly influenced by the experience of mass working class struggle in Belgium than any other Marxist thinker:

'The difference is that the mass strikes of the 1890's were spontaneous movements born of a revolutionary situation, of an intensification of the struggle, and of the extremely excited energy of the masses. They were not spontaneous in the sense of being chaotic, aimless or leaderless. On the contrary the leadership was in complete agreement with the masses...it felt close to the pulse-beat of the masses, adapted themselves to them, and was nothing but the conscious expression of their feelings and strivings.'[32]

She was beginning to develop the theory of the revolutionary general strike. However the defining moment in this intellectual growth,

---

[32] Luxemburg, Rosa (1928) Complete Works.

rooted in the experience of the oppressed, was the wave of mass strikes that brought Tsarist Russia to its knees in 1905. A new phenomenon had been defined, here the mass revolutionary strikes of the masses became alive and they manifest themselves in a new form of democracy known as the 'soviet' or workers council which grew out of this spontaneous activity:

'Instead of the hollow schema of political 'action' carried out at the behest of the highest party authorities to a cautious plan, we see a bit of life pulsing with flesh and blood which cannot be cut out of the great frame of the revolution, because it is connected to all the odds and ends of the revolution by a thousand veins.'

Rosa developed her argument...

'The mass strike is merely the form of the revolutionary struggle at a given moment, and every shift in its relation to the contending forces, in party development and class divisions, and in position to the counter-revolution. All this immediately affects the strike action in a thousand invisible and scarcely controllable ways...

Therefore In other words the Russian revolution...is the way in which the proletarian masses move, the 'form' taken by the proletarian struggle in the actual revolution.'[33]

She had articulated the theory of the general strike in a new way, a revolutionary paradigm. However the Russian 1905 insurrection was physically defeated and then the October 1917 revolution would stutter towards disaster a 'degenerated revolution' to coin Trotsky's phrase. So by the late 1920's the international proletariat were at best leaderless or betrayed by both the Reformists and the

---

[33] Luxemburg, Rosa. (1906) The Mass Strike, the Political Party and the Trade Unions.

collapsing Third International. Then 1929 and the Wall Street Crash, the world descends into barbarism: Recession and emergent fascism with only a small core of revolutionary communists to guide the masses through this crisis to what; the death agony of capitalism? There was a need to link again the economic and political elements of the proletarian armoury into a shining weapon of revived class warfare. Leon Trotsky provided the method required in the 'Transitional Programme'[34] The essence of Trotsky's methodology was the need to create 'a bridge' between the concrete daily struggles of workers which are known as 'minimalist demands' and the ultimate goal, the revolutionary triumph of the masses, a 'maximalist demand'. His task was to reinvigorate for different historical circumstances the theory of Marx, Engels and Luxemburg and to apply this theory to the last period of capitalism; Late-Capitalism. Trotsky argues:

'It is necessary to help the masses in the process of their daily struggle to find the bridge between present demands and the socialist program of the revolution. This bridge should include a system of transitional demands, stemming from today's consciousness of wide layers of the working class and the unalterable leading to one final conclusion: the conquest of power by the proletariat.'

- ibid

Why is this relevant today, simply because Trotsky had realized that the era of 'progressive capitalism' as an epoch had come to an end. Therefore the capacity of the bourgeoisie to meet 'minimal' demands was becoming limited, because of the Recession. Today we are in a similar situation

---

[34] Trotsky, L (1938) The Death Agony of Capitalism and The Tasks of The Fourth International

as the logic of Late-Capitalism has created another shattering Recession, the ruling class cannot meet the economic demands of the working class, indeed it must attempt to smash the working class to bail-out a crisis which is inherent within its own system capitalism; over-accumulation leading to a decline in the rate of profit. What is more their need to accumulate capital which 6 paradoxically leads to these crises has now put the survival of the planet at risk as catastrophic climate change is impacting globally.

Throughout the world revolutions and mass strikes are the response of the proletariat and their allies. The Marxist line is to synthesis the lessons Marx, Engels, Luxemburg and Trotsky learnt and reinvent them in the context of today's struggles. We learnt from Marx the need to seize state power, from Engels the necessity to unify the political and economic struggles; Rosa taught us the nature of the revolutionary road and Trotsky how to conduct the struggle during a Recession.

The Syndicalists, alternatively, see the General Strike as an end-in itself and so haven't understood Luxemburg's theory of the spontaneous Mass Strike which is that it creates interplay with party organization, transforming it in the process while allowing new forms of mass democracy to develop. The Reformists have long ago renounced working class 'self-activity'. Finally Rosa and Trotsky illustrate the way ahead today:

'In any great mass movement of the proletariat, a great number of political and economic factors coincide. To attempt to keep them separate would be a put them in a detrimental state' [35]

---

[35] Rosa Luxemburg Collected Works

and Trotsky[36]:

'The General Strike does ask before all classes in the nation. Who will rule?'

The proletariat and their allies, many poets and artists, or the anonymous super-rich.

---

[36] Trotsky, L. (1974) Writings 1938-39.

What are the theoretical disputes between Marxists and Anarchists?

'The world political situation as a whole is chiefly characterised by a historical crisis in the leadership of the proletariat. The economic prerequisite for the proletarian revolution has already been achieved.

...the bourgeoisie sees no way out' [37]

Trotsky wrote these words in an epoch very similar to the present. The world was deep in economic recession, the banks crumpling, the bourgeoisie trembling but the masses not making that next step to fulfil its world historical task and overthrow the rotting system which had created the objective conditions for its own demise. For:

'What the bourgeoisie therefore produces, above all, are its own grave-diggers. Its fall and the victory of the proletariat are equally inevitable.'[38]

So what is the most effective method in realizing the overthrow of capitalism? Two main traditions have existed in the consciousness of the advanced strata of the proletariat which will be generalized to the broad mass of the oppressed in a revolutionary situation: Marxism and Anarchism. There has developed a division between Marxists and anarchists which is often characterized by 'voluntarism' verses 'socialism', this is however to misunderstand the divide. Indeed the leading thinker of modern anarchism, Mikhail Bakunin like Karl Marx

---

[37] Leon Trotsky, (1938) *The Death Agony of Capitalism and the tasks of the Fourth International.*

[38] Karl Marx and Frederick Engels, (1848) *Manifesto of the Communist Party.*

supported the Paris Commune of 1871, the first time in history the working class had overthrown the state machinery of the bourgeoisie and created a workers' system. A significant modern libertarian thinker Noam Chomsky has commented:

'The consistent anarchist...will be a socialist, but a socialist of a particular sort; a libertarian socialist.'[39]

Although communists and anarchists aspire to a final goal which is a classless society without a state because the state apparatus is an instrument of class domination there are genuine methodological differences. These differences are routinely suggested to be firstly, the need of the 'autonomists' to 'rescue' Marx from Lenin and a second argument as made by Marshall[40] ' of a 'prophetic' claim by Bakunin that Marx was 'an advocate of state communism' that was 'vindicated by the verdict of history' as 'Stalinism'. Unlike other forms of Marxism, autonomist Marxism emphasises the ability of the working class to force changes to the organization of the capitalist system independent of the state, trade unions or political parties. Therefore they are centred instead on self-organized action outside of the traditional organizational structures of the proletariat with a focus on particularly 'abstentionism from work' and 'direct action'. Hence Herbert Marcuse argued:

---

[39] Noam Chomsky: (1970) "Introduction", in Daniel Guérin, *Anarchism (Monthly Review)*.

[40] Peter Marshall, (2008) Demanding *the Impossible: a History of Anarchist Thought*.

'Socialist solidarity is "autonomy", self-determination begins at home, and that is with every I and the We whom I choose.'[41]

The autonomists are therefore not 'rescuing' Marx from Bolshevik theoretical errors, but instead confusing the collective power of the proletariat with bourgeois individualism, an argument which is symptomatic of some Liberal commentators. Here is the source of the methodological problems; the autonomists or the Bakuninists do not have a coherent Marxist analysis of the human situation and condition. But rather they stray into seeking solutions like a lumpenproetariat 'refusal to work' as a tool of social transformation or the petty-bourgeois deviationism of 'propaganda by deed' as argued for by Bakunin. George Woodcock in his major work on Anarchism reflected:

'No conception of anarchism is further from the truth than that which regards it as an extreme form of democracy. Democracy advocates the sovereignty of the people .Anarchism advocates the sovereignty of the individual.'[42]

This cult of the atomised individual who is alienated and mute or as a revolutionary who commits acts of individual violence as opposed to the working class in a dialectical relationship with the vanguard party. Nevertheless the most advanced theoretician of vanguardism, Lenin, argued:

---

[41] Herbert Marcuse quoted in Luke Cooper (2011) *The problem of autonomism*

[42] George Woodcock (1962) *Anarchism.*

'We do not differ from the anarchists on the question on the abolition of the state.'[43]

So where do anarchists stand today on the questions of the relationship of theory and practice, class and party. One of their most advanced thinkers, David Graeber, argues consistently against organisation when he writes:

'The very notion of direct action, with its rejection of a politics which appeal to governments to modify their behaviour, in favour of physical intervention against state power in a form that itself prefigures an alternation – all emerges from the libertarian tradition.'[44]

Extrapolating from this perspective all manifestations of 'direct action' are a sort of new society incarnate, but as Alex Callinicos said 'the state will not leave us alone'. Revolutionaries cannot simply 'dream' that practice by practice alone without challenging the institutions of capitalism will create a communistic society. This is not simply a question of exegesis because the state is a body of armed people. Leon Trotsky encapsulated the problem with sharp clarity:

'To renounce the conquest of power is voluntarily to leave the power with those who wield it, the exploiters.'[45]

Therefore two questions remain a) how do we organize and b) can the state evaporate as a result of embryonic 'free zones' of one kind of or another created by counter-cultures or 'direct action'. The

---

[43] V.I. Lenin (1917) *The State and Revolution*.

[44] David Graeber (2002) *The New Anarchists*.

[45] Leon Trotsky (1973) *The Spanish Revolution*.

former is a debate which has its origins in the collapse of the First International, the debate between Marx and Bakunin and its ramifications and the second in a debate which is current in the anti-capitalist movement around 'horizontalism' and 'verticalism' which is a term which misconstrues the nature of the revolutionary party.

Firstly the controversy between Marx and Bakunin must be understood as their conflicting perspectives on the State. Significantly Marx saw the state was not inherently bad, but could be utilised by the proletariat in a transitional period between capitalism and a mature communist society which would be without class or state. He called this intermediate phase 'the dictatorship of the proletariat', what has become known as a 'workers' state'. György Lukács argued that this period was one of 'non-government' by which he meant that the state was in the possession of the majority and only in a position of rule or 'government' over the minority, the bourgeoisie. Marx envisaged that the proletariat would use the state apparatus to crush their oppressors; but that once this had been accomplished it would become redundant:

'To achieve its liberation it employs means which will be discarded after its liberation. ' [46]

Simply because once the masses control the 'means of production' through workers committees or as they were known in Russia as 'soviets' private property in the context of commodity production will cease. The requirement for an instrument of class domination will evaporate as production will not be driven by the need to accumulate profit and reinvest it endlessly 'accumulation for the sake of accumulation' (Marx) but the needs of human beings and therefore

---

[46] Karl Marl (1875) *Conspectus of Bakunin's State and Anarchy.*

their environment. Communism is the 'withering away of the state' (Engels) in the context of 'direct democracy' where production is planned for human need not driven by the insatiable drive to reproduce 'Capital'. Hence we can see the Marx did not believe human nature was 'fixed' but was the product of its socio-economic relations and therefore in a process of mutability. For Marx:

'The production of ideas, of conceptions, of consciousness, is at first interwoven with the material activity and material intercourse of men, the language of real life.'[47]

There is a material and social base of consciousness and it necessarily changes as this base does. Our consciousness, in the last instant, is a 'reflex' of socio-economic forces.

Here is the major philosophical difference with Bakunin who believed that there was a fixed 'human nature' which we must reconnect with:

'Man is himself nothing but nature...nature envelopes, permeates constitutes his whole existence.'[48]

Therefore for Bakunin human nature is not the product of social and economic forces, but in a tradition which has been seen as emanating from Taoism by some anarchists. Marshall quotes Chuang Tzu:

'Horses live on dry land, eat grass and drink water. When pleased, they rub their necks together. When angry, they turn round and kick up their heels at each other. Thus far only do their natural dispositions carry them. But bridled and bitted, with a plate of metal

---

[47] Karl Marx (1844) *The German Ideology*.

[48] Mikhail Bakunin (1973) *Bakunin on Anarchy*.

on their foreheads, they learn to cast vicious looks, to turn the head to bite, to resist, to get the bit out of the mouth or the bridle into it. And thus their natures become depraved. [49]

For horses substitute human beings, thus humanity has somehow became separated from its true nature, its 'moral law' has been corrupted by the State. Therefore Bakunin argues:

'I speak of the justice which is based solely upon human conscience...which translates into simple equality.'   - ibid.

These positions are quite different. Marx understands humans as beings who change and evolve through an objective material process, one of dialectical contradictions, qualitative leaps which manifest themselves as revolutions. Bakunin rather perceives Humanity in need of a return to a utopian 'nature', which can only be attained through insurrection triggered by individual acts of revolutionary violence.

We can see, therefore, that different philosophical positions informed the political differences which separated the Marxists from anarchists in their formative period. These profound disagreements create organisational problems. Today anarchists and autonomists reject organization in favour of 'networks' of individuals who coalesce around social 'issues' , this has been renamed 'horizontalism'. In these quarters there is an antipathy towards the Marxist-Leninist tradition where there is a relationship between cadres of committed revolutionaries who are organized in a vanguard Party which

---

[49] Peter Marshall (2008) *Demanding the Impossible: a History of Anarchist Thought.*

intervenes in the class struggle with the working class and has a democratic dialectical relationship with that class. Tony Cliff argues from a neo-Trotskyist [50]perspective that:

'The revolutionary party must conduct a dialogue with the workers outside it. [It] should not invent tactics out of thin air, but put as its first duty to learn from the experience of the mass movement and then generalise from it... Marxists [should] give a conscious expression to the instinctive drive of the working class to reorganise society on a socialist basis.'[51]

Cliff's earlier ambivalent relationship with Leninism can be seen in his 1959, *Rosa Luxemburg*:

'For Marxists, in the advanced industrial countries, Lenin's original position can such less serve as a guide than Rosa Luxemburg's, notwithstanding her overstatement on the question of spontaneity.'[52]

But Lenin presents us with an argument which is more cogent than this when he maintains:

---

[50] Orthodox Trotskyists apply Trotsky's 'method' rather than a literal interpretation to the present material conditions of capitalism while neo- Trotskyists claim to have developed that methodology intrinsically beyond Trotsky's original theoretical positions, some of which they consider to be flawed. Tony Cliff is the best known proponent of neo-Trotskyism, but some Marxists would argue that his tendency has vacillated on a number of central questions of theory.

[51] Tony Cliff (1996), *Trotsky on Substitutionism*.

[52] Tony Cliff (1959 ed) *Rosa Luxemburg*.

'Class political consciousness can be brought to the workers only from without, that is, only from outside the economic struggle, from outside the sphere of relations between workers and employers. The sphere from which alone it is possible to obtain this knowledge is the sphere of relationships of all classes and strata to the state and the government, the sphere of the interrelations between all classes.'[53]

Without politically conscious intervention by a revolutionary cadre workers' struggles will be merely economic. We can clearly understand that Lenin is arguing for a method of organisation which is quite complex. There are anarchist currents and spontaneity within the proletariat but the masses must be politically organised. This is the dialectic of class and party, spontaneity and organization. Lenin describes the nature of this dialectical process with the clarity of a revolutionary imbued by scientific socialism his ideas are an example of Marxian praxis[54]:

'A development that repeats, as it were, stages that have already been passed, but repeats them in a different way, on a higher basis ("the negation of the negation"), a development, so to speak, that proceeds in spirals, not in a straight line; a development by leaps, catastrophes, and revolutions; "breaks in continuity"; the transformation of quantity into quality; inner impulses towards development, imparted by the contradiction and conflict of the various forces and tendencies acting on a given body, or within a

---

[53] Lenin (1902) *What Is To Be Done?*

[54] György Lukács argued the task of political organization is to establish professional revolutionary discipline over everyday political praxis, designing the form of mediation best suited to clear interactions between theory and practice.

given phenomenon, or within a given society; the interdependence and the closest and indissoluble connection between all aspects of any phenomenon (history constantly revealing ever new aspects), a connection that provides a uniform, and universal process of motion, one that follows definite laws — these are some of the features of dialectics as a doctrine of development that is richer than the conventional one.'[55]

Hence Marxists reject autonomism and anarchism philosophically and organizationally arguing that:

'It is only in revolutionary struggle against the capitalists of every country, and only in union with the working women and men of the whole world, that we will achieve a new and brighter future-the socialist brotherhood of the workers.'[56]

---

[55] Lenin (1972) *Collected Works vol 38* Philosophical Notebooks.

[56] Alexandra Kollontai, (1917) *Our Tasks*.